CENGA   ...ng·

Short Stories for Students, Volume 1

STAFF

Kathleen Wilson, *Editor*

Tim Akers, Pamela S. Dear, David M. Galens, Jeffrey W. Hunter, Dan Jones, John D. Jorgenson, Marie Lazzari,
Jerry Moore, Deborah A. Stanley, Diane Telgen, Polly Vedder, Thomas Wiloch, *Contributing Editors*

Jeff Chapman, *Programmer/Analyst*

Greg Barnhisel, Stephan Dziemianowicz, Tim Engles, Mary Beth Folia, Christopher Giroux, Cynthia Hallett, Karen
Holleran, Jennifer Hicks, Logan Hill, Heidi Johnson, Tamara Kendig, David Kippen, Maryanne Kocis, Rena Korb,
Kim Long, Harvey Lynch, Thomas March, Carl Mowery, Robert Peltier, Elisabeth Piedmont-Marton, Trudy Ring,

Judy Sobeloff, Michael Sonkowsky, Anne Trubek, Julianne White, Janet Witalec, *Contributing Writers*

Susan Trosky, *Permissions Manager*
Kim Smilay, *Permissions Specialist*
Sarah Chesney, *Permissions Associate*
Steve Cusack, Kelly A. Quin, *Permissions Assistants*

Victoria Cariappa, *Research Team Leader*
Michele LaMeau, Barbara McNeil, Maureen Richards, *Research Specialists*
Laura C. Bissey, Julia C. Daniel, Tamara C. Nott, Tracie Richardson,
Norma Sawaya, Cheryl L. Warnock, *Research Associates*

Mary Beth Trimper, *Production Director*
Shanna Heilveil, *Production Assistant*

Cynthia Baldwin, *Production Design Manager*
Pamela A. E. Galbreath, *Senior Art Director*

Barbara J. Yarrow, *Graphic Services Manager*
Pamela Reed, *Photography Coordinator*
Randy Bassett, *Image Database Supervisor*

and inclusion in the publication of any organization, agency, institution, publication, service, or individual does not imply endorsement of the editors or publisher. Errors brought to the attention of the publisher and verified to the satisfaction of the publisher will be corrected in future editions.

This publication is a creative work fully protected by all applicable copyright laws, as well as by misappropriation, trade secret, unfair competition, and other applicable laws. The authors and editors of this work have added value to the underlying factual material herein through one or more of the following: unique and original selection, coordination, expressions, arrangement, and classification of the information.

All rights to this publication will be vigorously defended.

Printed in the United States of America.
10 9 8 7 6 5 4 3 2

Araby

James Joyce

1914

Introduction

"Araby" is one of fifteen short stories that together make up James Joyce's collection, *Dubliners*. Although Joyce wrote the stories between 1904 and 1906, they were not published until 1914. *Dubliners* paints a portrait of life in Dublin, Ireland, at the turn of the twentieth century. Its stories are arranged in an order reflecting the development of a child into a grown man. The first three stories are told from the point of view of a young boy, the next three from the point of view of an adolescent, and so on. "Araby" is the last story of the first set, and is told from the perspective of a boy just on the verge of adolescence. The story takes its title from a real festival which came to Dublin in 1894 when Joyce was twelve years old.

Joyce is one of the most famous writers of the Modernist period of literature, which runs roughly from 1900 to the end of World War II. Modernist works often include characters who are spiritually lost and themes that reflect a cynicism toward institutions the writer had been taught to respect, such as government and religion. Much of the literature of this period is experimental; Joyce's writing reflects this in the use of dashes instead of quotation marks to indicate that a character is speaking.

Joyce had a very difficult time getting *Dubliners* published. It took him over ten years to find a publisher who was willing to risk publishing the stories because of their unconventional style and themes. Once he found a publisher, he fought very hard with the editors to keep the stories the way he had written them. Years later, these stories are heralded not only for their portrayal of life in Dublin at the turn of the century, but also as the beginning of the career of one of the most brilliant English-language writers of the twentieth century.

Author Biography

James Joyce was born on February 2, 1882, the oldest often children born to John and Mary Joyce. Joyce's father, even though he was a good-natured man, was a drinker who wasted the family's resources. The Joyce family moved constantly, and Joyce became familiar with the sight of a pawnbroker's redemption slips and eviction notices.

In spite of his family's lack of money, Joyce was sent to Clongowes Wood College—a Jesuit Catholic boarding school—when he was six years old. Upon arrival, Joyce was asked his age, to which he replied, "Half-past six," which became his nickname for the rest of that year. Later, he went to another Jesuit school, Belvedere College, where he began to show his brilliance as a writer, winning several national competitions. Joyce spent the money he received from these competitions very quickly, celebrating with his large family at dinners in restaurants and redeeming some of his mother's possessions from the pawnbroker. Joyce was always painfully aware that he, being the oldest son, was given a good education and other privileges that his younger brothers and sisters could not receive.

When Joyce went to University College in Dublin, he began to rebel against his Catholic upbringing. Although successful in academic life, he found the unsophisticated narrowness of Irish politics and the arts stifling. After graduation, he met Nora Barnacle from Galway, Ireland, who would become his lifelong companion. Joyce was opposed to the institution of marriage, and he knew that he and Nora could not live together in Dublin without being married. So, after his mother's death in 1904, Joyce and Nora left Ireland to live the rest of their lives in continental Europe: first in Pola, in the former Yugoslavia; then Trieste, Italy, where their children Giorgio and Lucia were born; then Zurich, Switzerland, during the First World War; and finally, Paris. It was only after he left Ireland that Joyce was able to begin writing about his native country, and the stories in *Dubliners*, including "Araby," were written in his first years away, although they were not published until 1914.

During these years on the continent, Joyce supported his family by teaching English and holding a variety of other jobs, including managing an English theater troupe and working at a bank. He continued to write, but experienced only scattered commercial success. With the publication of his novel *Ulysses* in 1922, however, he reached a level of financial stability that enabled him to begin writing full-time. In the following years, his already poor eyesight got progressively worse, and he underwent several eye operations. Also during this period, Joyce's daughter suffered a nervous breakdown and was hospitalized in a sanitarium in Zurich. In 1931, after 27 years of living together, Joyce and Nora were finally married. They were afraid that after Joyce died, Nora would be left with no rights to his estate. Joyce died on January 13, 1941, following surgery for an ulcer. He was 58 years old.

"Araby" opens on North Richmond street in Dublin, where "an uninhabited house of two storeys stood at the blind end, detached from its neighbours in a square ground." The narrator, who remains unnamed throughout the story, lives with his aunt and uncle. He describes his block, then discusses the former tenant who lived in his house: a priest who recently died in the back room. This priest has a library that attracts the young narrator, and he is particularly interested in three titles: a Sir Walter Scott romance, a religious tract, and a police agent's memoirs.

The narrator talks about being a part of the group of boys who play in the street. He then introduces Mangan's sister, a girl who captivates his imagination even though he rarely, if ever, speaks with her. He does stare at her from his window and follow her on the street, however, often thinking of her "even in places the most hostile to romance." While in the marketplace on Saturday nights, for example, he uses her image to guide him through the thronging crowd who yell their sales pitches and sing patriotic Irish ballads. He becomes misty-eyed just at the thought of her and retreats to the priest's dark room in order to deprive himself of other senses and think only of her.

Finally, Mangan's sister speaks to him. She asks if he will be attending a church-sponsored fair that is coming soon to Dublin—a bazaar called Araby. He is tongue-tied and cannot answer, but when she tells him that she cannot go because of a retreat that week in her convent, he promises to go and bring her a gift from the bazaar. From then on he can only think of the time when he will be at the fair; he is haunted by "the syllables of the word Araby." On the night he is supposed to attend the fair, his uncle is late returning home and he must wait to get money from him. He gets very anxious, and his aunt tells him that he may have to miss the bazaar, but his uncle does come home, apologetic that he had forgotten. After asking the boy if he knows a poem entitled "The Arab's Farewell to His Steed," the uncle bids the boy farewell.

The boy takes a coin from his uncle and catches a train to the fair. Araby is closing down as he arrives and he timidly walks through the center of the bazaar. As he looks at the few stalls that are still open, he overhears a conversation between an English shop-girl and two young men. Their talk is nothing but idle gossip. The shop-girl pauses reluctantly to ask the boy if he wishes to buy anything, but he declines. As he walks slowly out of the hall amid the darkening of the lights, he thinks that he is a "creature driven and derided by vanity" and his "eyes burned with anguish and anger."

Mangan

Mangan is the same age and in the same class at the Christian Brothers school as the narrator, and so he and the narrator often play together after school. His older sister is the object of the narrator's confused feelings.

Mangan's Sister

Mangan is one of the narrator's chums who lives down the street. His older sister becomes the object of the narrator's schoolboy crush. Mangan's sister has no idea how the narrator feels about her, however, so when they discuss Araby, the bazaar coming to town, she is only being polite and friendly. She says she would like to go to the bazaar but cannot because she has to attend a school retreat that weekend. The narrator promises to buy her something at the bazaar if he goes, but it is unlikely that she takes this promise seriously. While on the one hand the narrator describes her romantically, he also describes her in reverential terms which call to mind the Virgin Mary. This dual image description of Mangan's sister represents the religious and romantic confusion of the narrator.

Mrs. Mercer

Mrs. Mercer is the pawnbroker's widow who waits at the house for the narrator's uncle, perhaps to collect money that he owes her. Joyce includes her character to show that the uncle is unreliable in the payment of his debts.

Narrator

The narrator of this story is a young, sensitive boy who confuses a romantic crush and religious enthusiasm. All of the conflict in this story happens inside his mind. It is unlikely that the object of his crush, Mangan's sister, is aware of his feelings for her, nor is anybody else in this boy's small world. Because the boy's thoughts only reveal a part of the story, a careful reader must put together clues that the author gives. For example, the narrator mentions that the former tenant of the house he shares with his aunt and uncle was a priest, a representative of the Catholic church, who left behind three books which became important to the narrator. One is a romantic adventure by Sir Walter Scott; one is a religious pamphlet written by a Protestant; and the third is the exciting memoirs of a French policeman and master of disguise. These three books are not what a person would expect a Catholic priest to have in his library. So if this priest has non-religious literature in his library, then how devout can an average churchgoer be expected to be? This turns out to be the case for the narrator, who confuses religious idealism with romance.

Media Adaptations

- *The Dead*, a film based on one of the stories in *Dubliners*, was directed by John Huston (starring his daughter, Anjelica) and produced by Vestron Pictures in 1987.

The boy confuses the religious and secular worlds when he describes himself at the market with his aunt. He bears the chalice—the Communion cup—through a "throng of foes." He also describes Mangan's sister in terms often associated with the Virgin Mary. For the narrator, then, an ordinary grocery-shopping trip becomes a religious crusade, and a pretty girl down the street becomes a substitute for the Mother of God. The boy fuses together religious devotion for the Virgin Mary with his own romantic longing.

Joyce is famous for creating characters who undergo an epiphany—a sudden moment of insight —and the narrator of "Araby" is one of his best examples. At the end of the story, the boy overhears a trite conversation between an English girl working at the bazaar and two young men, and he suddenly realizes that he has been confusing things. It dawns on him that the bazaar, which he thought would be so exotic and exciting, is really only a commercialized place to buy things. Furthermore, he now realizes that Mangan's sister is just a girl who will not care whether he fulfills his promise to buy her something at the bazaar. His conversation with Mangan's sister, during which he promised he would buy her something, was really only small talk —as meaningless as the one between the English girl and her companions. He leaves Araby feeling ashamed and upset. This epiphany signals a change in the narrator—from an innocent, idealistic boy to an adolescent dealing with harsh realities.

Narrator's Aunt

The narrator's aunt, who is a mother figure in the story, takes the narrator with her to do the marketing. When it seems as though the uncle has forgotten his promise to the narrator that he could go to the bazaar, she warns the boy that he may have to "put off" the bazaar "for this night of Our Lord." While this statement makes her seem strict in a religious sense, she also exhibits empathy for the boy's plight. She pleads his case when the uncle forgets about the boy's plans to go to Araby.

Narrator's Uncle

The narrator's uncle seems self-centered and very unreliable. When the narrator reminds him that he wants to go to the bazaar, he replies, "Yes, boy, I know." But on the Saturday evening of the bazaar, he has forgotten, which causes the narrator to arrive at the bazaar very late. When the uncle finally shows up, he has been drinking, and as the boy leaves for the bazaar he begins reciting the opening lines of the poem, "The Arab's Farewell to his Steed." Joyce's characterization of the uncle bears resemblance to his own father, who liked to drink and was often in debt. Joyce's inclusion of Mrs. Mercer, the pawnbroker's widow who waits for the uncle to return, suggests that the uncle owes money.

Themes

A sensitive boy confuses a romantic crush and religious enthusiasm. He goes to Araby, a bazaar with an exotic, Oriental theme, in order to buy a souvenir for the object of his crush. The boy arrives late, however, and when he overhears a shallow conversation a female clerk is having with her male friends and sees the bazaar is closing down, he realizes that he has allowed his imagination to carry him away. He leaves without a souvenir, feeling foolish and angry with himself.

Alienation and Loneliness

The narrator never shares any of his feelings concerning Mangan's sister with anyone. He isolates himself from his friends, who seem terribly young to him once his crush begins, and from his family, who seem caught up in their own world. Mangan's sister is also completely unaware of the narrator's feelings for her. Consequently, when he suddenly realizes how foolish he has been, his anger at himself is intensified by his alienation from everyone and the resulting feeling of isolation.

Change and Transformation

The narrator experiences emotional growth—changing from an innocent young boy to a disillusioned adolescent—in the flash of an instant.

This insight occurs through what Joyce called an "epiphany," which is a moment of intense insight and self-understanding. Although the narrator suddenly understands that he has allowed his feelings to get carried away, this understanding makes him neither happy nor satisfied. If anything, he is very angry at himself for acting foolishly. This realization marks the beginning of his maturation from a child into an adult.

God and Religion

At the beginning of the story, the narrator sees himself as a religious hero and sees Mangan's sister as the living embodiment of the Virgin Mary. He has not yet learned how to separate the religious teachings of his school with the reality of his secular life. Part of his understanding at the end of the story involves his finally separating those two aspects of his life. He realizes that the church-sponsored bazaar is just a place to buy trinkets, that Mangan's sister is just a girl, and that he. himself is just a boy. It is not clear at the end of the story what impact the narrator's epiphany will have on his religious beliefs. Joyce's own disillusionment with Catholicism, however, lends credence to the possibility of the boy adopting a cynical attitude toward his religion.

Style

Through the use of a first person narrative, Joyce communicates the confused thoughts and dreams of his young male protagonist. Joyce uses this familiarity with the narrator's feelings to evoke in readers a response similar to the boy's "epiphany"—a sudden moment of insight and understanding—at the turning point of the story.

Topics for Further Study

- Joyce once said that in *Dubliners* he intended "to write a chapter of the moral history of Ireland, because Dublin seemed to him to be at the "centre of paralysis." What do you think he meant by that? If you were to write a chapter of the moral history of your country, which city would you choose to be at the center? Why?

- A recurring theme in many of the stories in *Dubliners* is a longing for escape expressed through fantasies of flight to someplace Eastern and exotic. What place represents the unknown to you? Research this place and discuss whether it is truly exotic and mysterious or just different.

- Catholicism figures prominently in much of Joyce's work. Compare the influence of the Catholic Church in Ireland at the turn of the century and today. Would the themes of religious confusion and doubt in "Araby" create controversy in modern-day Ireland?

Point of View

The first-person point of view in "Araby" means that readers see everything through the eyes of the narrator and know what he feels and thinks. If the narrator is confused about his feelings, then it is up to the readers to figure out how the narrator really feels and why he feels that way, using only the clues given by the author. For example, when the narrator first describes Mangan's sister, he says that "her figure [is] defined by the light from the half-opened door." In other words, she is lit from behind, giving her an unearthly "glow," like an angel or supernatural being such as the Virgin Mary. Readers are left to interpret the meaning behind the narrator's words, because the boy is not sophisticated enough to understand his own longings.

Symbolism

The symbolism Joyce includes also helps readers to fully understand all of the story's complexities. The former tenant of the narrator's house, the Catholic priest, could be said to represent the entire Catholic church. By extension, the books left in his room—which include non-religious and non-Catholic reading—represent a feeling of ambiguity toward religion in general and Catholicism in particular. The bazaar, Araby, represents the East—a part of the world that is exotic and mysterious to the Irish boy. It could also represent commercialism, since it is really just a fundraiser used to get people to spend money on the church. Mrs. Mercer, the pawnbroker's widow, represents the uncle's debt and irresponsibility; she too could represent greed and materialism. To the narrator, Mangan's sister is a symbol of purity and feminine perfection. These qualities are often associated with the Virgin Mary, who also symbolizes the Catholic church. While the boy is at Araby, the various, and often contrasting, meanings of these symbols converge to produce his epiphany.

Stream of Consciousness

Joyce is famous for using a stream-of-consciousness technique for storytelling. Although stream of consciousness does not figure prominently in "Araby," a reader can see the beginnings of Joyce's use of this technique, which he used extensively in his subsequent novels, *Ulysses* and *Finnegans Wake*. A major feature of stream-of-consciousness storytelling is that the narration takes place inside the mind of main characters and follows their thoughts as they occur to them, whether those thoughts are complete sentences or not. Although this story uses complete sentences for its storytelling, the narration takes place inside the boy's mind. Another feature of stream-of-consciousness narration is that the narrator's thoughts are not explained for the reader. This is true of "Araby" as well, especially during and after the boy's epiphany.

While Dublin, Ireland, has seen change since the turn of the twentieth century, when Joyce wrote "Araby," many of the conditions present then remain today. In 1904, all of Ireland was under British control, which the Irish resented bitterly. The nationalist group, Sinn Fein (part of which later became the Irish Republican Army—the IRA), had not yet formed, but Irish politics were nonetheless vibrant and controversial. The question of Irish independence from Britain was one of primary importance to every citizen.

Ireland's major religion, Roman Catholicism, dominated Irish culture. Many families sent their children to schools run by Jesuit priests (like the one the narrator in "Araby" attends) and convent schools run by nuns (like the one Mangan's sister attends). Folklore, fairy tales, and homespun stories —told and retold for generations—provided a common form of family entertainment. Many turn-of-the-century stereotypes about the Irish came from their cultural traditions. Some common ones included large families, drunkenness, poverty, and imaginative storytelling.

The large families seen in Ireland at the turn of the century stemmed largely from the Catholic religion. Divorce went against church doctrine, and abortion and birth control were considered mortal sins. It was also a mortal sin for husbands and wives to refuse to engage in sexual relations to prevent having more children. As a consequence, it was not unusual for Irish Catholic families at the turn of the century to be quite large. While the modern Catholic church does not exercise quite as much influence, these issues still figure strongly in Irish culture today.

There were no televisions or radios for entertainment at the turn of the century. Many homes had no electricity and were heated only by a central fireplace. Therefore, the custom of storytelling after dinner (or "tea") was one common form of entertainment. In light of these living conditions, it is clear why an event like the bazaar in "Araby" could cause such great expectations.

The stereotype of the drunken Irishman arose partly in response to the poverty experienced by the majority of people in Ireland after the Great Potato Famine of the 1840s. Beer was cheap and often more sanitary than the water. The Irish were also famous for their whiskey, which many still claim to be the finest in the world. The local public house— or pub—was the central gathering place of the village, and also served as a small hotel for weary travelers. People were certain to find warm hospitality, good beer and mutton stew, and good stories around the hearth to lift their spirits there. In the evening, the men would gather at the pub to drink, talk of politics or sports, and hear music. Unfortunately, this led to many men wasting their families's meager resources, thereby reinforcing the stereotype of the drunk, irresponsible Irishman. The narrator's uncle in "Araby," who keeps the narrator and the pawnbroker's widow waiting before coming home drunk, fits this mold.

In larger cities like Dublin and Belfast, many Irish cultural stereotypes have disappeared as Ireland has become modernized. In many parts of Ireland, though, poverty still exists and the pub is still the town's social center.

Critical Overview

Joyce had a hard time getting *Dubliners* published. Although he wrote the stories between 1904 and 1906, and some of them were published in magazines, the entire collection was not published in book form until 1914. The book was first accepted for publication by the Grant Richards publishing company in 1906, but after a long controversy and many arguments between Joyce and the editors over changes the company wanted to make to the stories, they withdrew their offer to publish.

The second company that accepted the manuscript for publication in 1909 was Maunsel and Company, a Dublin publisher. This company had second thoughts about publishing the work as well, and in 1912 they destroyed the proofs that Joyce had corrected. This left Joyce extremely bitter. Finally, in 1914, Grant Richards, the company that originally accepted the manuscript for publication again agreed to publish Joyce's work.

This troubled road to publication influenced the early reviews and criticism of *Dubliners*. According to Robert Scholes and A. Walton Litz, the editors of the 1996 edition of *Dubliners* published by Viking Press, these stories were mostly dismissed by early critics as Joyce's "apprentice" work, or given a secondary place as "skillful but depressing 'slices' of Dublin life."

Dubliners was published four months after the publication of Joyce's next work, *A Portrait of the Artist as a Young Man,* Its reception was overshadowed by excitement and attention given to both *Portrait* and early chapters of *Ulysses,* which Joyce was publishing in magazines around the same time. Many readers during this time found *Portrait* —a revealing story of a troubled young man searching for his place in life—far more interesting than the stories in *Dubliners.* For many years Joyce's problems with publishers and printers were discussed more frequently than the stories themselves.

Early reviews of *Dubliners* set the pattern for subsequent critical discussion. Many critics protested against the sordid incidents related in some of the stories and the overall pessimistic tone of the collection. These critics complained that these stories lacked a "point," and that they were merely anecdotes or sketches without any definite structure. At least two reviewers found the longer stories the least satisfactory because Joyce did not sustain a "mood" in them as he did in the shorter pieces.

The turning point in *Dubliners* criticism came in the 1940s and 1950s, when critics began to find in Joyce's work interesting and novel connections between such elements as tone, atmosphere and action. While some critics still focus on these stories as evidence of the young Joyce developing his distinctive style, or emphasize that Joyce provides a truthful, skillful depiction of life in Dublin at the turn of the century, the criticism now encompasses a wide range of interpretations and appreciation. Most critics now agree that *Dubliners* stands on its own merits as a great work by one of the most important writers of the twentieth century.

What Do I Read Next?

- *Dubliners* is the complete collection of 15 short stories by James Joyce, all loosely connected as each one describes people living in Dublin, Ireland, at the turn of the century.

- *A Portrait of the Artist as a Young Man.* This first novel by Joyce describes the early life of Stephen Dedalus, a sensitive, intelligent young man struggling to understand life and his role in it.

- *Ireland: A Terrible Beauty*(1975). A

collection of photographs by Jill Uris, accompanied by text written by her husband, author Leon Uris. This book not only gives an overview of the history of the Emerald Isle, but also shows off the beauty of the island in many exquisite photographs.

- *Ireland: Art into History*(1994). This book, edited by Brian P. Kennedy and Raymond Gillespie, traces the history of Ireland through its art, from prehistoric times to the present. It presents both art and history, without being too academic.

- *The Common Chord: Stories and Tales*(1947), by Frank O'Connor, is a collection of short stories from this famous Irish writer. Written from the point of view of a young boy, O'Connor's stories are funny, truthful, and many times touched with an edge of sadness.

- *The Commitments*(1988) and *Paddy Clarke Ha Ha Ha*(1993), both by Irishman Roddy Doyle, are novels set in contemporary working-class Ireland. *The Commitments* describes the efforts of Jimmy Rabbitte to start a band which covers American soul songs of the 1960s by such greats as Otis Redding and Sam Cooke.

Paddy Clarke Ha Ha Ha gives the reader a look at life through the eyes of a ten-year-old boy in modern-day Ireland.

Sources

Scholes, Robert and A. Walton Litz, editors. *Dubliners: Text, Criticism, and Notes*, Penguin, 1996.

Further Reading

apRoberts, R. P. "The Palimpsest of Criticism; or, Through a Glass Eye Darkly," in *The Antioch Review*, Vol. XXVI, 1966-67, pp. 469-89.

> apRoberts's sarcastic attack on what he sees as Harry Stone's excessively reaching reading of "Araby." Where Stone holds that "Araby" must be seen in light of Joyce's other writing, apRoberts insists that it is self-contained.

Brown, Homer Obed. *James Joyce's Early Fiction*, Archon, 1975.

> A study of the methods of Joyce's early fiction (primarily *Dubliners)* and the themes the work explores.

Levin, Harry. *James Joyce*, New Directions, 1960.

> A general discussion of Joyce's work and his techniques, written in 1941, the year of Joyce's death.